Table of Contents

Sweet Potato Matcha Milkshake
Matcha Hot Chocolate
Matcha Ice Cream Float
Coconut Matcha Iced Tea
Matcha Mango Smoothie
Tropical Matcha Iced Tea
Herbal Matcha Iced Tea
Matcha Lemon Ice
Matcha Tapioca Bubble Tea
Holiday Matcha Egg Nog
Matcha Cosmopolitan
Matcha Beer

An Introduction to Matcha

Image by <u>Vegan Baking</u> via <u>Flickr</u>

What is Matcha?

You might be wondering, "Isn't matcha just another word for green tea?"

Yes and no.

Matcha is green tea with a distinctive twist. It is the same old green tea leaf we know and love, but ground into an extraordinarily fine powder. This powder isn't steeped in water, like a whole green tea leaf. Rather, the powder is whisked into the water and allowed to dissolve. Typically, only higher quality green tea cultivars are processed into matcha. Other powdered green teas exist, but they are not considered matcha. They are cheaper overall, come from lower quality tea cultivars and contain parts of the plant that do not dissolve in water. If it doesn't dissolve, it's not matcha.

If you are recently discovering matcha, you have probably seen images of powdery heaps and opaque, foamy beverages. The substance has a mysterious air about it. Why does it look so different from every other type of tea that graces our breakfast tables? To modern Western sensibilities, the only powdered tea comes in instant on-the-go packets that only require you to dump and stir.

Asia is no stranger to powdered tea, and we're not talking about instant teas here. Actually, quite the opposite from instant. Entire ceremonies, rituals, and political dynamics have evolved around powdered tea; matcha has very close ties to Zen Buddhism. To this day, more than a thousand years later, the ceremonial tea preparation etiquette devised by Buddhist monks continues to be practiced throughout China and Japan.

It isn't just used for tea drinks either; matcha has become very popular as a green coloring additive as well as a delightful flavoring ingredient. It can be found in pastries, donuts, candies, ice cream, bread and pasta. Strolling down the neon streets of Tokyo, matcha can be spotted on virtually any convenience store shelf.

Where does it come from?

Matcha originated in China between 800 and 1000 C.E. Buddhist monks transformed the traditional green tea preparation by grinding up their leaves and whisking the fine powder together with water. It traveled by trade routes to Japan around 1100 C.E. and took a firm hold of the nation, starting with Buddhist monks and eventually attracting the refined tastes of the upper class. Many international tea experts consider only Japanese matcha blends to be "true" matcha.

The Health Benefits of Matcha

If you have ever glanced at the supermarket checkout counter's magazine racks, you have probably noticed the flashy, attention-grabbing health magazine headlines. Every week a new magazine invites you to discover the natural wonders of green tea: they'll tell you it can boost weight loss, treat cancer, and perform otherworldly miracles. It all sounds too good to be true!

Well, in this instance the magazines may not be lying to you. And, as it turns out, the health benefits of green tea are exponentially stronger due to its high quality and highly concentrated format.

Traditional Medicinal Uses of Matcha

Centuries ago in China, matcha caught public attention as a valuable medicinal drink. To this day, research continues to demonstrate that matcha-drinking communities have a significantly lower incidence of cancer and other major health problems.

Due to its noteworthy caffeine content, it was commonly employed as a stimulant and diuretic (something which flushes fluids out of the human body). Matcha was hailed as a prevention and treatment for many maladies, ranging from heart problems to fatigue and fevers.

Matcha's tannin content makes it an effective astringent (something which draw bodily tissues close together), so it was often used externally to dry out wounds, sores, and fungus-affected skin.

Building Blocks of Matcha

To understand why matcha stands apart from your average mug of green tea, you have to look more closely at the particular cultivation, harvest, preparation and consumption style that defines it.

The best quality matcha is produced from young leaves, harvested from the top of the green tea bush. These leaves can be processed into a finer, more soluble powder and allow for a more pleasant drinking experience. Young leaves aren't just selected for texture – they are ideal because the plant prioritizes these leaves in terms of nutrition. To promote growth, a greater quantity of nutrients is directed towards young leaves. This makes matcha tea significantly more nutritious than other types of green tea. Some tea experts estimate that one cup of matcha tea contains up to ten cups of regular green infusions.

By drinking good quality matcha, you consume whole tea leaves. Dipping a teabag into a cup does infuse hot water with many beneficial compounds. Sadly, since you don't end up eating the tea leaves, you will still waste many of the helpful fibers, nutrients and compounds. Drinking matcha means you leave none of the good stuff behind.

So, what *is* the good stuff?

- Antioxidants
- Caffeine
- Catechins
- Chlorophyll
- Essential amino acids
- Flavonoids
- Polyphenols
- Tannins
- Vitamins A, B, C, E, and K, Zinc, Magnesium

While scientific debates still surround many supposedly beneficial substances, it is widely accepted that matcha has some powerful healing and cleansing properties. This acceptance reaches far beyond superstition: it is all based on solid scientific evidence. Even better: all of the proven benefits comes from studies on green tea, meaning that matcha can dramatically boost these positive effects.

Let's delve into the real, tangible health benefits of drinking matcha.

Strengthen the Body and Mind

Considering the range of vitamins and minerals provided by matcha, it is basically like a delicious, drinkable multivitamin. By drinking 3-5 cups per day, you can reach the daily required intake of many trace vitamins. These vitamins are necessary to keep you in tip-top shape.

B-complex vitamins improve digestion, alleviate intestinal upset, keep the mind sharp, and fortify and stimulate the growth of hair and nails. Vitamin C enhances immunity and helps you resist sickness. Vitamin E, often referred to as the anti-aging vitamin, creates a barrier against the sunshine's ultraviolet (UV) rays, keeping your skin youthful and unharmed. Polyphenols, which also work as antioxidants, prevent blood sugar spikes after eating and also protect your skin from harmful UV rays.

High quantities of natural fiber are present in matcha because the whole tea leaf is utilized. Fiber is essential for healthy digestion.

Fat Burning Power

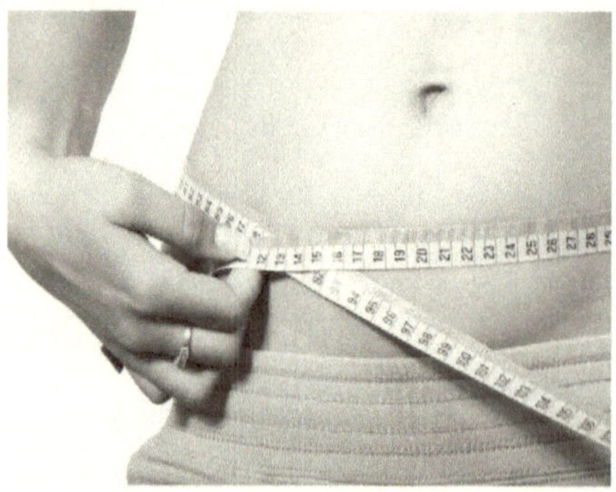

Research has largely demonstrated that the catechins in matcha can help people maintain healthy body weight and actively promote weight loss. They can do away with old fat storage cells, as well as redirect resources to build muscle as opposed to fat.

Due to the catechin content, matcha burns up a fair amount of calories during digestion. It does so by increasing internal body temperature incrementally, thereby upping your body's activity level and burning fat.

With the added kick of caffeine thrown into the mix, your metabolism will be working harder than ever before to work away the extra pounds.

Don't underestimate the power of staying cool and collected while trying to lose weight. Anxiety is considered to be a major contributing factor to obesity. Drinking matcha calms the nervous system and reduces stress and anxiety. Having a soothing cup of lovingly-prepared matcha tea is a far better habit than stress eating!

Try adding a midday tea break to your routine to ward away stress and bad dietary habits. A simple, wholesome cup of matcha has a low calorie count – but beware the mixed matcha drinks! When you purchase a matcha latte, matcha frappucino, or any other matcha-based beverage, there will be added calories from sugar, milk, and whatever else makes it taste so darn delicious.

Moreover, matcha is also thought to help weight loss programs by acting as an all-natural appetite suppressant.

Kick Your Metabolism into Gear

Given that matcha encourages weight loss, you would probably expect it to crank up your metabolism rate as well. You're right!

A study published by the American Journal of Clinical Nutrition in 1999 showed us that drinking matcha can up your body's daily caloric expenditure to 20% or 30% - a normal daily rate is 8% to 10% of calories burned. Wow!

Diet is certainly important for effective weight loss, but so is exercise. Another publication released by the same journal demonstrated that drinking green tea right before exercising can help you burn up to 25% more body fat. That's pretty significant! And remember, that was about green tea – the effect will be more all the more noticeable with matcha.

Cleanse Your Body

Chlorophyll and antioxidants make matcha an ideal detoxifying agent. The green tea plants cultivated for matcha are shade-loving; growing in the shade encourages slower growth and greatly increased chlorophyll production. Thus, the best of the best matcha powder should be a dark, rich, lively green.

If you're stumped trying to remember that 5th grade science class when you learned what chlorophyll does, let me give you a hand: chlorophyll absorbs sunlight and aids in photosynthesis. It supplies plants with nutrition and gives them their characteristic green pigmentation.

There was a time when the medicinal properties of chlorophyll were overhyped by the media, so it is often viewed with suspicion now. However, this little molecule has a lot to offer us! It is a known detoxifying agent, able to attach itself to free radicals and dangerous toxins swimming around the body. Once attached, chlorophyll neutralizes its target. For this reason, chlorophyll-rich matcha is strongly associated with detoxification and cancer prevention.

High levels of antioxidants, including catechins, aid in chlorophyll's spring cleaning work.

Keep Calm and Drink Matcha

Thanks to one very valuable chemical component of matcha, L-theanine, it is the perfect tea to soothe your fried nerves and give you peace of mind. L-theanine is an amino acid found in tea which creates a calming effect on the brain. This, in turn, can help alleviate anxiety manifested as physical tension. L-theanine can also protect your brain from overfiring neurotransmitters and harmful chemicals which lead to cell degradation and make you more vulnerable to anxiety.

You may think the caffeine would counteract any noteworthy calming effects. As a matter of fact, caffeine working in combination with L-theanine can do wonders for mental cognition and focus.

Luckily, matcha has just the right amount of caffeine, not too little, not too much. One cup of matcha contains about 1/3 the caffeine found in a cup of black tea, and as little as 1/10 the amount found in the average cup of coffee. This makes it the perfect pick-me-up! You want a small jolt of alertness, energy, and mental focus? Grab a cup of matcha and forget about jitters, heart palpitations, anxiety, and coffee breath. Of course, if consumed in unreasonably large doses, matcha can also cause the classic caffeine-related side effects.

This combined effect of energy, focus, and calming is why monks were the first to adopt matcha. They drank matcha to put themselves in the perfect state for meditation: relaxed, with sharp mental clarity

Reduce the Risk of Cardiovascular Disease

Cardiovascular disease is the leading cause of death worldwide. As we continue to look for solutions, green tea has exhibited great promise as a natural preventative treatment.

Low-density lipoprotein (LDL), also known as "bad cholesterol," cowers in the wake of green tea's catechin content. Matcha is even more strongly enriched than green tea with this great antioxidant.

Matcha's flavonoids have anti-inflammatory properties, meaning that they reduce the swelling and inflammation of bodily tissues. In turn, this enables a vigorous and unobstructed blood flow and promotes a healthy heart. Circulation is also aided by the numerous matcha compounds which grab onto fat molecules and keep them safely away from the bloodstream; rather, they push these fats through your digestive tract and out of your system.

Prevent Diabetes

Diabetes is a metabolic disease that is defined by high blood sugar levels. Type II diabetes occurs when cells no longer react to insulin levels and, as a result, inadequate amounts of insulin are produced by the body. Green tea slows down the digestion of food in the mouth and stomach by stalling the activity of certain digestive enzymes. It is also able to get insulin wherever it is immediately needed, bypassing all the potential obstacles and storage areas. Don't let you insulin be misappropriated again, drink matcha!

High blood sugar levels conspire with free radicals in the body to cause severe, life-threatening cardiovascular conditions. The antioxidants in matcha seek out free radical, cling to them, and redirect them to safer spaces.

Achieve Immortality

Matcha is the closest humans have come to creating an elixir for immortality. Think about all the other benefits you have just read about. It totally makes sense that, if matcha can improve health in so many different ways, it can also help you live a longer and healthier live overall. What sort of problems do people experience with advancing age? Matcha helps maintain healthy body weight, boost metabolism, cleanse the body, reduce anxiety, and more – it is even thought to prevent cancerous cells and heart disease.

The data backs up this logical reasoning. A 2006 publication in the Journal of the American Medical Association found that, for their subjects, green tea consumption is inversely related to mortality. This means that drinking green tea was a good predictor for longer life.

Matcha Drink Recipes

Image by [Akuppa John Wingam](#) via [Flickr](#)

Matcha can be prepared in the traditional style, whisking into water, or paired with other ingredients to create delicious, colorful, and inspired drinks. Take a look at our collection of original recipes and learn the many ways you can take your daily dose of matcha. The recipes include:

Traditional drinks

Milk-based drinks

Fruit drinks

Alcoholic drinks

Pay close attention to preparation methods! Matcha can be prepared in a variety of ways, and the method chosen for each drink is important to have a scrumptious final product. You will need to have the following equipment on hand:

- Wooden, bamboo or electric handheld whisk
- Mesh sifter
- Chasaku - bamboo matcha measuring spoon
- Ceramic mug or tea bowl (does not affect flavor of traditionally prepared matcha)

Traditional Matcha

The classic, simple cup of matcha tea.

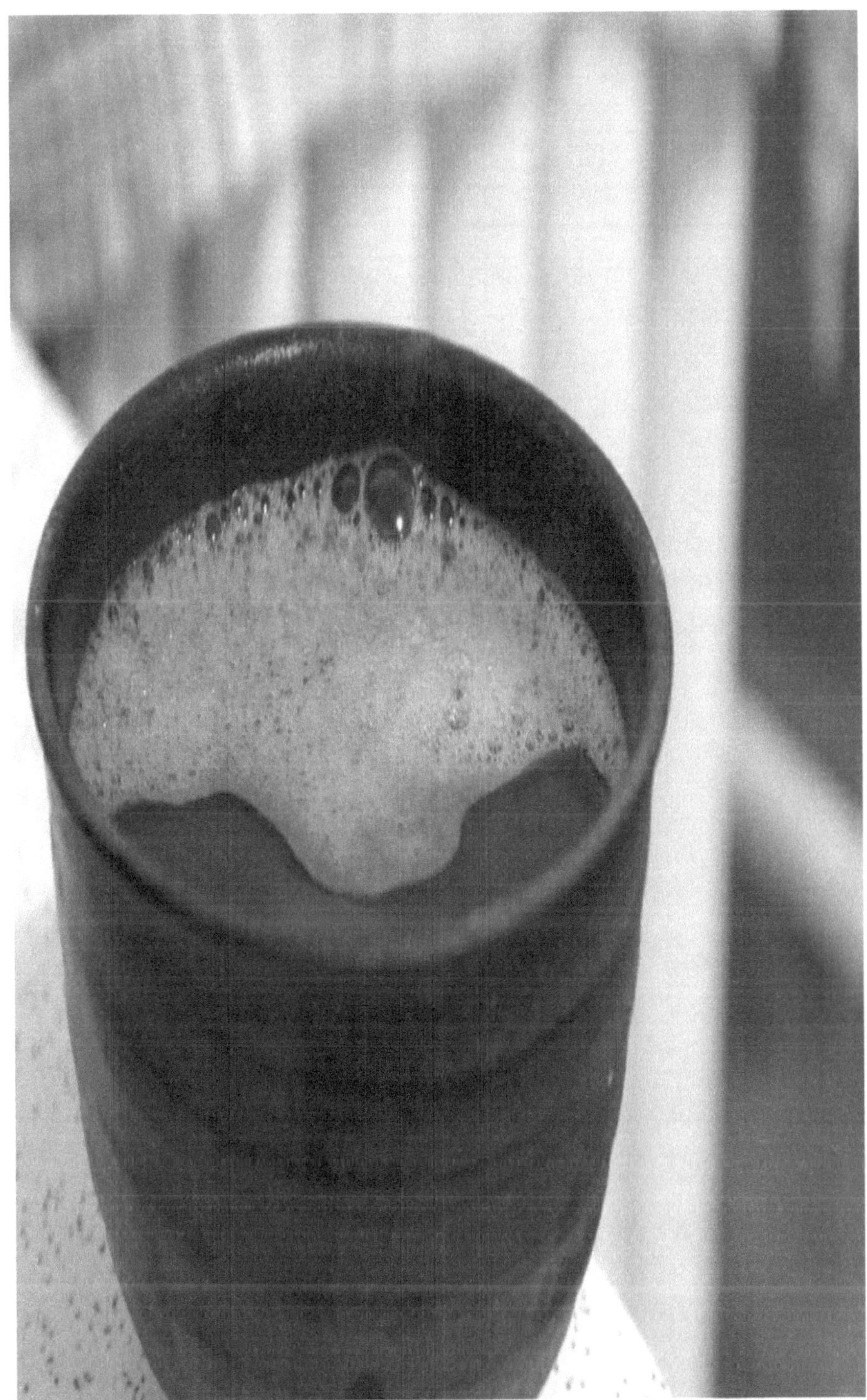

Image by <u>Jigme Datse Rasku</u> via <u>Flickr</u>

Ingredients

2 chasaku or 1 teaspoon matcha powder

1/2 cup water

Preparation

1. Boil water. Remove from heat. Ideal temperature is between 160-175°F.
2. Warm ceramic mug or tea bowl by pouring in one tablespoon of heated water.
3. Sift matcha powder over clean paper towel or plate.
4. Measure matcha powder and add to mug or tea bowl.
5. Add heated water.
6. Whisk gently from left to right, not in circles – it's all in the wrist! Steadily increase speed.
7. Whisk surface of matcha for perfect consistency.

Power-Packed Mini Matcha

Condensed matcha goodness for a quick boost.

Mini Matcha. Image by Mike via Flickr

Ingredients

4 chasaku or 2 teaspoons matcha powder

1/2 cup water

Preparation

Follow steps 1-7 of the Traditional Matcha recipe.

Elegant Red Bean Matcha

A sweet, stylish version of the traditional matcha drink.

Image by EJstanz via Flickr

Ingredients

2 chasaku or 1 teaspoon matcha powder per half cup of water

Water

2 tablespoons cooked and sweetened azuki beans (red beans)

Preparation

1. Boil water. Remove from heat. Ideal temperature is between 160-175°F.

2. Warm ceramic mug or tea bowl by pouring in one tablespoon of heated water.

3. Sift matcha powder over clean paper towel or plate.

4. Measure matcha powder and add to mug or tea bowl.

5. Add heated water.

6. Whisk gently from left to right, not in circles. Steadily increase

speed.

7. Whisk surface of matcha for perfect consistency.

8. Top with azuki beans.

Matcha Latte

A cool twist on a coffee house favorite

Image by [cgc76](#) via [Flickr](#)

Ingredients

2 chasaku or 1 teaspoon matcha powder per cup

1/3 cup water

2/3 cup milk, soy milk, or hazelnut milk

1 tablespoon honey per cup

Preparation

1. Boil water Remove from heat. Ideal temperature is between 160-175°F.

2. Warm ceramic mug or tea bowl by pouring in one tablespoon of heated water.

3. Sift matcha powder over clean paper towel or plate.

4. Measure matcha powder and add to mug or tea bowl.

5. Add heated water.

6. Whisk gently from left to right, not in circles. Steadily increase speed.

7. Add milk and whisk vigorously.

8. Add honey as desired.

9. Whisk surface of matcha for perfect consistency.

Matcha Spice Latte

A matcha latte with a spicy zing.

Image by <u>Alpha</u> via <u>Flickr</u>

Ingredients

2 chasaku or 1 teaspoon matcha powder

1/3 cup water

3-4 thin slices ginger root per cup

2/3 cup milk, soy milk, or hazelnut milk

1/8 teaspoon cinnamon

1/8 teaspoon nutmeg

1 tablespoon honey per cup

Preparation

1. Boil water with ginger slices. Remove from heat. Ideal temperature is between 160-175°F.

2. Follow steps 2-7 of the Matcha Latte recipe.

3. Add cinnamon, nutmeg, ginger and vanilla to matcha while whisking vigorously.

4. Add honey as desired.

5. Whisk surface of matcha for perfect consistency.

6. Sprinkle pinches of matcha powder and cinnamon on top.

Breakfast Matcha Yogurt Smoothie

Start your day right with this nutritious, fruity blend.

Image by Stephan Hochhaus via Flickr

Ingredients

2 chasaku or 1 teaspoon matcha powder

1/2 cup Greek yogurt

3 chopped strawberries

1/4 cup raspberries

1/4 cup blueberries

5-6 Ice cubes

Preparation

1. Put all ingredients in blender and blend on medium speed until smooth and free of chunks.

2. Pour into glass and enjoy.

Strawberry Banana Matcha Smoothie

This healthy smoothie will fuel you throughout the day.

Image by Meal Makeover Moms via Flickr

Ingredients

2 chasaku or 1 teaspoon matcha powder

1 peeled banana (overripe works)

¼ cup chopped strawberries

1/2 cup milk or soymilk

1 teaspoon honey if desired

Preparation

1. Add all ingredients to blender. Blend on high speed until smooth and free of chunks.

2. Pour and enjoy.

Dreamy Creamy Matcha Milkshake

Have an insistent sweet tooth? This milkshake will satisfy.

Image by <u>Mariko</u> via <u>Flickr</u>

Ingredients

6 chasaku or 3 teaspoons matcha powder

1 cup vanilla ice cream

1/2 cup milk, soy milk, or almond milk

1/4 cup fresh whipped cream

Preparation

1. Put all ingredients in blender. Blend on high speed until smooth, free of chunks.

2. Dollop fresh whipped cream and sprinkle matcha powder for decoration.

3. Serve immediately.

Sweet Potato Matcha Milkshake

Sounds like a wacky combination? This milkshake is rich, naturally sweet, and unique.

Image by Emily C via Flickr

Ingredients

4 chasaku or 2 teaspoons matcha powder

1 cup sweet potato, peeled, cooked and mashed

1 cup vanilla ice cream

1/2 cup milk, soy milk, or almond milk

1/2 teaspoon ground cinnamon

1/8 teaspoon ground ginger

Preparation

1. Put all ingredients in blender. Blend on high speed until smooth, free of chunks.

2. Serve immediately.

Matcha Hot Chocolate

Curl up on a cozy winter evening with this reinvented classic.

Image by [Stephanie Bond](#) via [Flickr](#)

Ingredients

2 chasaku or 1 teaspoons matcha powder

1 teaspoon cocoa powder

1/2 teaspoon cinnamon

1 cup milk or vanilla soymilk

Marshmallows (optional)

Chocolate shavings (optional)

Whipped cream (optional)

Preparation

1. In a small pot, gently heat milk over low heat.

2. Whisk matcha powder, cocoa powder, and cinnamon together with warm milk.

3. Pour into mug and put marshmallows, chocolate shavings, and whipped cream on top if desired.

4. Serve warm.

Matcha Ice Cream Float

Skip the root beer and whip up this striking matcha float!

Image by Ippe Sukzuki via Flickr

Ingredients

2 chasaku or 1 teaspoon matcha powder

1/3 cup milk, soy milk, or almond milk

2 scoops vanilla ice cream

Preparation

1. Sift matcha powder over clean paper towel or plate.
2. Measure matcha powder and add to mug or tea bowl.
3. Add milk and Whisk gently from left to right. Steadily increase speed until all powder is dissolved.
4. Pour matcha into float glass.

5. Lightly whisk surface of matcha for perfect frothiness.

6. Add the ice cream scoops.

7. Serve immediately.

Coconut Matcha Iced Tea

A fresh, coconut flavored spin on matcha tea.

Image by <u>Liralen Li</u> via <u>Flickr</u>

Ingredients

2 chasaku or 1 teaspoon matcha powder

1/2 cup raw coconut water

1 teaspoon lime juice

2 small sprigs of mint

Preparation

1. Whisk together matcha, coconut water, and lime juice.

2. Serve over ice.

3. Decorate with sprigs of mint.

Matcha Mango Smoothie

Tastes like sunshine! Matcha pairs surprisingly well with thick, sweet mango juice.

Image by <u>Meal Makeover Moms</u> via <u>Flickr</u>

Ingredients

2 chasaku or 1 teaspoon matcha powder

1 cup fresh sliced mango

1/2 cup fresh sliced papaya

1/2 cup milk or soymilk

1/3 cup plain or vanilla yogurt

Preparation

1. Add all ingredients to blender. Blend on high speed until smooth and free of chunks.

2. Serve immediately.

Tropical Matcha Iced Tea

A fruity, citrusy beverage to keep you cool.

Image by Pen Waggner via Flickr

Ingredients

2 chasaku or 1 teaspoon matcha powder

1/2 cup raw coconut water

1/4 cup orange juice

1 tablespoon lime juice

1 tablespoon lemon juice

1/2 slice of pineapple

1 teaspoon honey

Cherry for decoration

Preparation

1. Whisk together matcha, coconut water, orange juice, lime juice, and lemon juice.
2. Stir in honey to taste.
3. Whisk surface of matcha for perfect consistency.
4. Serve over ice.

5. Wedge pineapple slice on the edge of the glass so it is partially submerged.

6. Place cherry on top for decoration.

Herbal Matcha Iced Tea

This cold, earthy beverage aims to refresh and replenish.

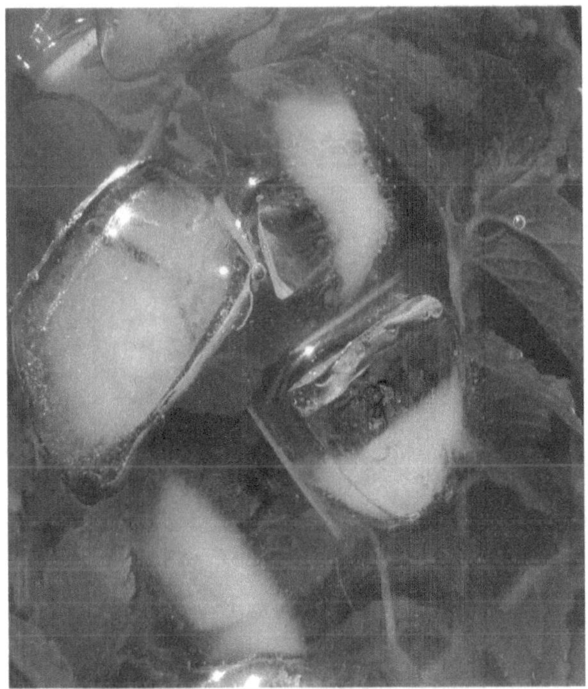

Image by S_A via Flickr

Serves 4

Ingredients

4 chasaku or 2 teaspoons matcha powder

4 tablespoons lemongrass

3 tablespoons peppermint

2 tablespoons grated ginger

2 teaspoons orange rind

1 teaspoon hibiscus

2 tablespoons honey

4 cups water

Preparation

1. Put water in a medium pot with lemongrass, peppermint, ginger, orange rind and hibiscus. Bring to a boil, then reduce to a simmer. Simmer for 20 minutes.

2. Strain herbs from water.

3. Whisk herbal infusion together with matcha powder.

4. Stir in honey to taste. Serve over ice.

Matcha Lemon Ice

An icy cold refreshment for hot summer days.

Serves 2

Ingredients

2 chasaku or 1 teaspoon matcha powder

3 cups water

1/4 cup lemon juice

4-5 thin lemon slices

6-8 thin cucumber slices

1/2 cup raspberries

2 tablespoons honey

Preparation

1. In a medium-sized pitcher, whisk together matcha powder, lemon juice, and room temperature water.

2. Stir in honey to taste.

3. Add lemon slices, cucumber slices and raspberries.

4. Chill for two hours in refrigerator or serve over ice.

Matcha Tapioca Bubble Tea

Get your matcha fix with the added fun of tapioca pearls.

Image by Cyclonebill via Flickr

Ingredients

6 chasaku or 3 teaspoons matcha powder

1 cup almond milk

1/3 cup tapioca pearls

20 drops stevia

Preparation

1. Cover tapioca pearls with water in a medium pot. Add 10 drops of stevia sweetener. Boil for 3 minutes, drain, and put in drinking glass.

2. Whisk together almond milk, matcha powder, and 10 drops stevia sweetener.

3. Pour matcha milk over tapioca peals.

4. Whisk surface of matcha for perfect consistency.

5. Serve chilled.

Holiday Matcha Egg Nog

This matcha drink captures all the festivity and flavor of the winter holidays.

Image by Christian Kadluba via Flickr

Ingredients

6 chasaku or 3 teaspoons matcha powder

3 egg yolks

2 cups whole milk

1 cup heavy cream

1/4 cup raw sugar

1/3 cup bourbon or rum

3 cloves

1 teaspoon ground cinnamon

1/2 teaspoon ground nutmeg

Preparation

1. Combine milk, cinnamon, nutmeg, and cloves in a medium

pot. Heat gently until boiling. Remove from heat.

2. Whisk sugar and egg yolks together until peaks form.

3. Stir the warm, spiced milk into the yolk mixture.

4. Heat gently and stir until thickened. Remove cloves and remove from heat. Let stand for half an hour.

5. Whisk in matcha powder and bourbon (or rum).

6. Chill and serve.

Matcha Cosmopolitan

A trendy feature for any cocktail party. Perfect for ladies' night!

Image by [seesternrea](#) via [Flickr](#)

Ingredients

1 chasaku or 1/2 teaspoon matcha powder

1 1/2 ounces vodka

1/2 ounce triple sec

1 teaspoon lime juice

1, thin 3-inch orange peel

Preparation

1. Fill shaker with ice and add matcha powder, vodka, triple sec, and lime juice. Shake for 1-2 minutes until the liquid is chilled and the powder has dissolved.

2. Strain liquid into martini glass.

3. Garnish with orange peel and enjoy.

Matcha Beer

Complementary bitter and sweet notes give this an outstanding flavor.

Image by Arnie Kim via Flickr

Ingredients

2 chasaku or 1 tablespoon matcha powder

3 tablespoons warm water

1, cold 14 ounce beer

Preparation

1. Whisk matcha powder with warm water until dissolved.
2. Add matcha mixture to beer and whisk until combined and frothy.
3. Enjoy cold.

www.ingramcontent.com/pod-product-compliance
Lightning Source LLC
Chambersburg PA
CBHW031811150726
47989CB00006B/2951